STEAM GUIDES IN

.TV Production

Judy Greenspan

Rourke
Educational Media
rourkeeducationalmedia.com

Scan for Related Titles and Teacher Resources

Before Reading:

Building Academic Vocabulary and Background Knowledge

Before reading a book, it is important to tap into what your child or students already know about the topic. This will help them develop their vocabulary, increase their reading comprehension, and make connections across the curriculum.

1. *Look at the cover of the book. What will this book be about?*
2. *What do you already know about the topic?*
3. *Let's study the Table of Contents. What will you learn about in the book's chapters?*
4. *What would you like to learn about this topic? Do you think you might learn about it from this book? Why or why not?*
5. *Use a reading journal to write about your knowledge of this topic. Record what you already know about the topic and what you hope to learn about the topic.*
6. *Read the book.*
7. *In your reading journal, record what you learned about the topic and your response to the book.*
8. *After reading the book complete the activities below.*

Content Area Vocabulary
Read the list. What do these words mean?

assemble
consists
creativity
dramas
encounter
equation
interpret
range
sequence
technique
technology
theory
transform

After Reading:

Comprehension and Extension Activity

After reading the book, work on the following questions with your child or students in order to check their level of reading comprehension and content mastery.

1. *What role do computers play in special effects?* (Summarize)
2. *What is the difference between a live broadcast and a pre-recorded show?* (Inferring)
3. *What is a green screen and how is it used?* (Asking questions)
4. *Can you name five people who are behind the scenes of a television program?* (Text to self connection)
5. *How is a television show rated?* (Asking questions)

Extension Activity

TV is an important part of our lives. We watch our favorite shows and even use it to play video games. With all the information you learned in the book, do you think you might be interested in a career in TV? Choose the most interesting job in the book and do some research on the Internet to find out more about the education you will need, the job duties required, and how long it will take you to obtain this career. Write down the pros and cons to see if a STEAM career in TV is right for you.

Table of Contents

Behind the Scenes ... and the Screen

This is a book about television. But it's not a book about watching television. You already know how to do that. It's more about what you don't watch on television. What you don't see. In fact, can't see. And maybe never even think about when you turn on your favorite show.

After all, TV seems so simple. There are hundreds of channels, thousands of shows, and we can watch what we want at the touch of a button.

However, television is more complicated than it appears. Just count the names in the credits at the end of a program. You can see that behind the scenes, television takes teamwork, **creativity**, hours of effort, and something more.

STEAM Fast Fact!

Tele means *far* or *far off* in Greek and *visio* means *seeing* in Latin. So television literally means seeing from a distance.

All of that fun stuff you watch on TV also depends on science and math. That may not seem obvious so let's say it another way. How about:

Surprised? Then let's find out how!

Let's start with some of the coolest things you see on TV—like special effects, for example. Want to make snow fall in summer? Send a stuntman flying through the air? Fill a room with smoke that doesn't make anyone cough? Sounds like magic, but it's science.

The Magic of Science? Or the Science of Magic?

The three most common states of matter are liquid, solid, and gas. The same matter can exist in all three states. To change matter from one state to another, we simply need energy.

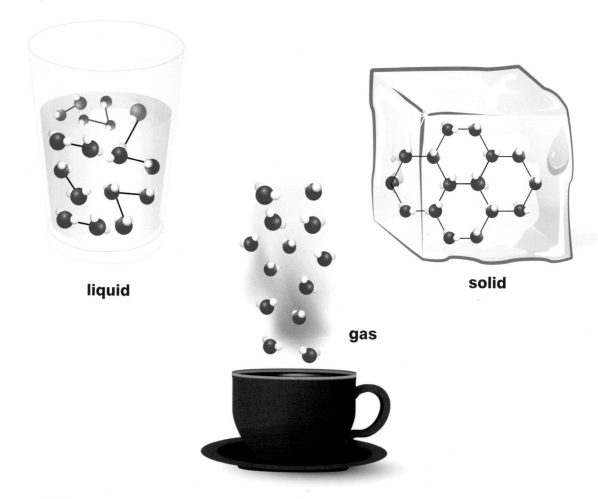

liquid

gas

solid

Take an ice cube. It's a solid. Add energy in the form of heat and that solid becomes a liquid. In this case, it becomes water. Add heat to the water and what happens? We create gas, or specifically steam.

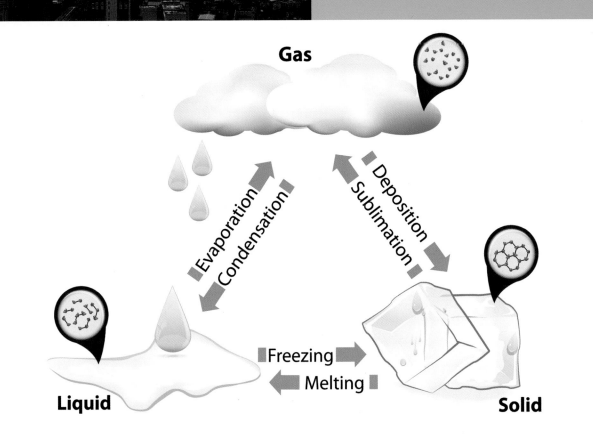

Gas

Evaporation
Condensation

Deposition
Sublimation

Freezing
Melting

Liquid

Solid

STEAM
Fast Facts!

Three most common states of matter and how to tell the difference:

Solid State: Volume and shape don't change.
Liquid State: Volume doesn't change but shape can.
Gas State: Both shape and volume can change.

SOLID   LIQUID   GAS

Matter: Everything that takes up space and has mass.

Particles: Microscopic units of matter. Electrons are particles.

Now let's take that science lesson and go behind the scenes of a TV show.

Suppose the director of the show wants her actors to sit in a smoky room. Or better yet, run through clouds of billowing smoke! On TV, that smoke has to look real. But behind the scenes, it's science in action.

To create fake smoke, we begin with a familiar **equation**:

$$\text{liquid} + \text{heat} = \text{gas}$$

In this case, the liquid is a harmless mixture, often called fog juice. We pour the fog juice into a smoke machine. The smoke machine adds heat and the heat creates gas. Our equation now looks like this:

**fog juice (liquid) + heat (smoke machine)
= fake smoke (gas)**

Gas expands, so, it doesn't take much fog juice to make a lot of fake smoke. It's harmless, of course. But on TV, that fake smoke looks scary!

Blowing smoke! The smoke machine makes it look real but this smoke is harmless.

STEAM Profile !

Gary Zeller

Chemist Gary Zeller combined his love of science with a flair for entertainment. He invented Zel Jel, a goopy substance to help stunt performers protect their skin during fire stunts. Zeller won an Academy Award for his creation in 1989.

You can create special effects through the magic of **technology** as well. That superhero flying through the air? All you need for this effect are computers and something called a green screen. But to see a green screen in action, you don't need a superhero.

A meteorologist is a scientist who studies the atmosphere. A television meteorologist is often the person giving the weather report, as well. On TV, meteorologists appear to be standing in front of large weather maps with moving graphics. But in reality, they are standing in front of a large green screen.

The weather maps are actually on computers. The computer is then programmed to place the map on anything green. This is a special effect called Chroma key. Chroma key is the **technique** used to electronically replace a specific color with another color or an image. In this case, the color green is replaced with the weather map.

Although we see a large map on television, the meteorologist is watching the maps on nearby monitors. He or she changes the images with a remote control. Good trick, right? But there's one catch. Meteorologists can't wear green! Can you guess why?

Television and Ducks. That's Right. Ducks!

Television shows such as **dramas** and sitcoms are almost always pre-recorded. That means the show is completed before it airs. But television news shows, like most sports events, air live.

You're watching as it's happening. Nothing is more exciting than live television, and behind the scenes, nothing is more unpredictable!

Why is Live TV like a Swimming Duck?

Because we don't see all the hard work that makes both looks so easy. In television, a team of people are working hard behind the scenes. And beneath that duck calmly swimming along? Two webbed feet are paddling like crazy!

Who Works in Television News?

When you watch television news, you see a few people on camera. But most of the people who make the newscast possible are working behind the scenes.

On Camera

news anchor

meteorologist

reporters

Behind the Scenes

news director

show director

executive producer

show producer

senior producers

producers

production assistants

news writers

camera operators

audio board operator

tape room operator

teleprompter operator

engineers

graphic artists

Live news reporters cover everything from crime to community events.

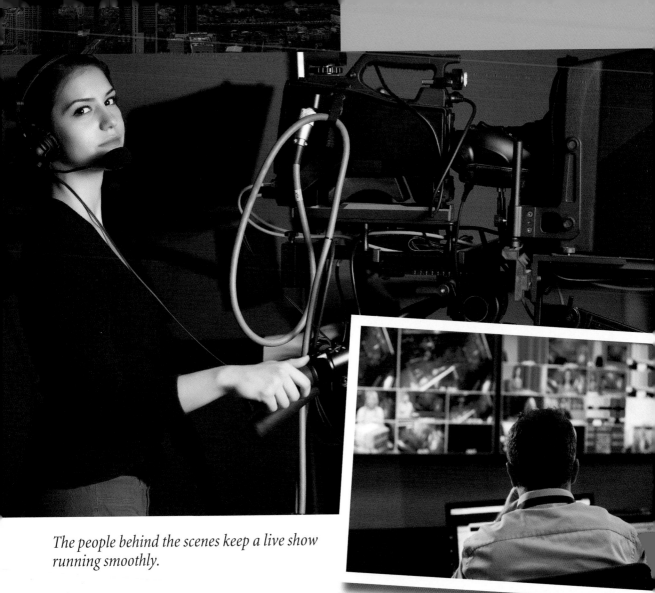

The people behind the scenes keep a live show running smoothly.

Every second counts in live TV. Split-second timing is one of the most important parts of a live newscast. Do you think anyone would notice if you showed up 45 seconds late for dinner? Probably not. But on live TV, 45 seconds late would feel like a long time!

A live newscast has to start on time. It has to end on time. And all the parts in between—weather, sports, news, commercials—are timed exactly. Computer software makes the math much easier but a show producer knows how to add and subtract minutes and seconds ... fast!!

STEAM in Action!

Let's see what it's like to plan a 15-minute newscast with three stories. First, before we can decide how long the stories will be, we have to subtract six minutes for commercials.

$$
\begin{array}{r}
15:00 \\
-\ 6:00 \\
\hline
9:00
\end{array}
$$

Now we have nine minutes left, but we also have to subtract a minute and a half for the opening music and introductions.

Remember though, subtracting minutes and seconds can get tricky. Nine minutes is not the same as 900.

Here's the difference:

$$
\text{not}\quad
\begin{array}{r}
900 \\
-\ 130 \\
\hline
770
\end{array}
\qquad
\text{but}\quad
\begin{array}{r}
9:00 \\
-\ 1:30 \\
\hline
7:30
\end{array}
$$

Since one minute = 60 seconds, another way to set up the equation is:

$$\begin{array}{r} 8:60 \\ -\ 1:30 \\ \hline 7:30 \end{array}$$

Either way, we have 7:30 left. We need :30 at the end of the show to say goodbye ...

$$\begin{array}{r} 7:30 \\ -\ :30 \\ \hline 7:00 \end{array}$$

... which leaves us a grand total of 7:00 for our three stories. Here's one way we can divide the remaining time:

Story 1:   3:00
Story 2:   2:30
Story 3:   1:30
         7:00

Our show looks well planned, but does that mean our plan will go well? Not necessarily! In news, anything can change and usually does. What then? Add, subtract ... and do it quickly! Producers need to think fast and have nerves of steel!

Seeing from Far Away

Television was a 20th century invention, but it was based on a 19th century discovery.

Did you know that every time you turn on your TV, you tap into invisible waves of energy? Called electromagnetic waves, they race through the air at the speed of light: 186,000 miles (300,000 kilometers) per second. That's fast enough to circle Earth seven and a half times! Years before television was invented, scientists discovered that electrical signals could be sent along this invisible force. This discovery would eventually lead to the invention of radio, sending sound through the air. After that, sending pictures and sound through television was only a matter of time!

By the mid 1930s most American families had a radio.

James Clerk Maxwell
1831 – 1879

Heinrich Hertz
1857 – 1894

An invention we watch all the time began with a discovery no one can see!

1864: Scottish physicist James Clerk Maxwell came up with a **theory** that said electromagnetic waves could travel through space.

1888: German physicist Heinrich Hertz proved him right by demonstrating that electromagnetic waves did exist. Hard to believe now, but Hertz did not think his discovery would be useful!

1900: Russian scientist Constantin Perskyi is said to have come up with the word television during the World's Fair. The name was in place, but the invention was still years away.

You already know a lot about electromagnetic waves. More than you may think. The electromagnetic spectrum **consists** of the seven main types of energy waves. We can only see one, visible light, but we **encounter** many others every day. For instance, you microwave your popcorn. Your bags are x-rayed at the airport. And radio waves bring us radio and TV.

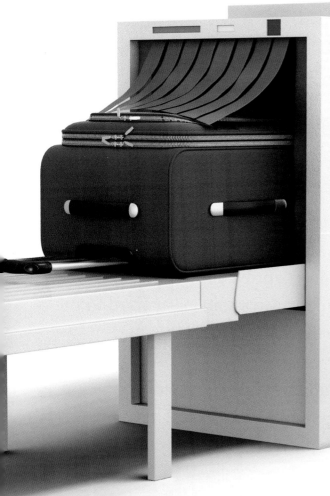

X-Ray machines allow airport security staff to see what's inside of every suitcase.

Electromagnetic Spectrum

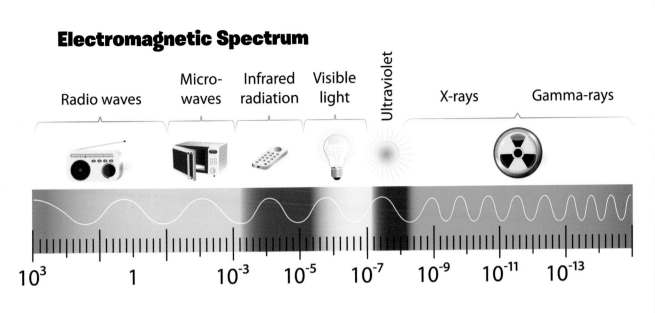

Radio waves | Micro-waves | Infrared radiation | Visible light | Ultraviolet | X-rays | Gamma-rays

10^3 1 10^{-3} 10^{-5} 10^{-7} 10^{-9} 10^{-11} 10^{-13}

Another word for spectrum is **range**. The electromagnetic waves on the spectrum are grouped by frequencies, ranging from lowest to highest. Frequency is the number of times a wave moves up and down per second. Frequency is measured by a unit called *hertz*—named after the scientist Heinrich Hertz. If a wave moves up and down 300 times in a second, we say it has a frequency of 300 hertz.

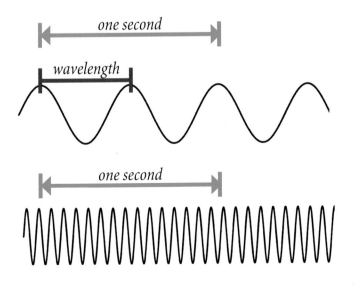

one second

wavelength

one second

Which wavelength has the faster frequency? Which wavelength has the slower frequency?

The science of sending the television signal to your TV is not simple. But basically, here's what happens:

1. The television camera and microphone **transform**, or change, pictures and sound into electronic signals.

2. The signals are carried at the speed of light as electromagnetic waves.

3. The signal is sent either through the air, or by cable, or bounced to a satellite and back to Earth.

4. Your television receives the signal. Based on the information it carries, your TV—with the help of your brain—puts all the pieces back together again. Now you can watch TV.

Science? Yes. But you'll be tempted to call what happens next pure magic.

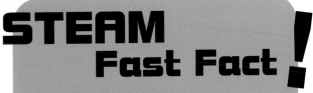

STEAM
Fast Fact!

Satellite TV is amazing. Satellite dishes are parked 22,000 miles (36,000 kilometers) above Earth's surface. Sound far? It is, but you know radio waves are fast. In one second, a TV signal can travel there and back four times!

It's All an Illusion

Now things get really interesting. It turns out that what we see on the television screen is actually an optical illusion. That means we're not seeing what we think we're seeing. Those moving images? They're not really moving! Instead, we're watching a **sequence** of thousands of individual pictures presented one right after the other. But they fly by so fast that our brains **interpret** everything together as a moving image.

STEAM in Action!

An Electronic Flipbook

24 pictures per second create the illusion of moving images on TV. At that rate, how many images are in a 30-minute show?

24 x 60 seconds =   1,440 pictures per minute

1,440 x 30 minutes = 43,200 pictures

Now for the second part of the magic: the pictures themselves are also an illusion. Each picture is actually made up of thousands and thousands of tiny dots called pixels. Your brain, however, is able to put all those dots together and **assemble** an image.

Let's try it.

Look at this image while you're holding the book. Now step back and look again from a distance. Can you see the image more clearly now? That's your brain, hard at work!

Your television does the rest of the work. The technology of creating an electronic flip book with pixilated images depends on the kind of television you have, but the idea is more or less the same for all of them.

Simply put, the television needs to turn millions of different colored pixels on and off, over and over again to recreate the images. Think of it like painting by numbers, except with pixels instead of paint.

There are only red, green, and blue pixels in color television. Scientists discovered long ago that the wavelengths of these three colors can be combined to create every color in the rainbow.

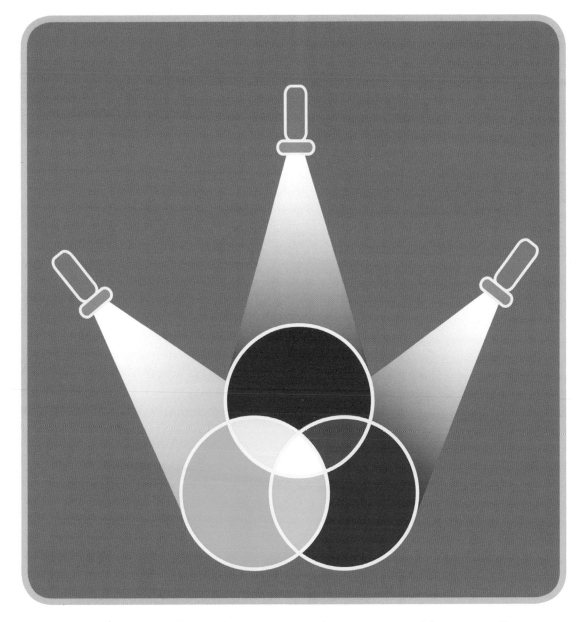

What are the colors in the rainbow? Just remember Roy G. Biv: Red, orange, yellow, green, blue, indigo, and violet.

As technology changes so does the shape of the television!

1931 television receiver

The first mass produced TV set, sold in 1946 and 1947

A family watching television in 1958

Modern televisions are so thin, we can hang them on the wall.

STEAM Profile !

Who invented television? More than one scientist can take credit but Philo Farnsworth was one of the most important. Back in 1920, he was only 14 when he was inspired by a row of potatoes! Plowing parallel rows of dirt in the field, he suddenly saw a way to send pictures "through the air." What if he created something that would break down pictures into parallel lines of electricity? Then he could send the lines of electricity through the air and put everything back together again on a screen. Wow, that's a lot of inspiration from a potato field! And it worked too. Eight years later he sent the world's first television image.

Philo Farnsworth

1906 – 1971

Relax, You're Using Binary Numbers

Can you believe that people once had to get up to change the television channel? Imagine having to walk all the way across the room! Luckily scientists corrected this problem by inventing the remote control. Remote controls operate on a number system called binary numbers.

Binary numbers, or base-2 numbers, are made up of only 0s and 1s.

For example, this is what the number 12 looks like in base-2: 00001100

Numbers in base two look confusing, unless you're a computer. Or a digital television. Or a remote control. Then 1s and 0s just mean on and off. Any combination of these numbers sends a different instruction.

When you press any button on your remote, a beam of infrared light streams toward your TV, sending a coded signal. For example, maybe 1010101 means volume up. 11100101 might mean change the channel.

Infrared light was discovered in 1800, long before television or remote controls were invented.

The remote also has a secret code so that you can only use it with your television. Crack that code, and you might be able to turn your neighbor's TV on and off!

STEAM Profile !

The Founding Father of the Couch Potato

Eugene Polley invented the first wireless remote, the Flashmatic, in 1955. Instead of infrared light, his early design shot a beam of visible light at a target on the TV. Unfortunately, sunlight hitting the same target tended to change the channels as well!

Rate That Show!

You've probably heard the expression, "the most highly rated show in television." But what does that mean? What exactly is a rating?

A television rating is a way to measure both who is watching TV and what they are watching. It is a percentage: the number of households (the people in one home) watching a show divided by the total number of households that have a television.

Rating = households watching a show ÷ by all households with a television

Ratings are important to advertisers. They pay a lot of money to place an ad on a highly rated show.

STEAM in Action!

Let's say there are ten homes with televisions, and in three of those homes, they are watching a show called *Amazing Animals*.

$$\frac{\text{3 homes watching } Amazing\ Animals}{\text{10 homes with a television}} = 3/10 \text{ or a rating of 30}$$

What if six of those ten homes are tuned into a different show called *Not Such Amazing Animals*? Which show is more highly rated?

$$\frac{\text{6 homes watching } Not\ Such\ Amazing\ Animals}{\text{10 homes with a television}} = 6/10 \text{ or a rating of 60}$$

Of course, in real life it's not possible to measure what millions of people are watching on television. That's why ratings are based on what's called a statistical sample. Nielsen chooses a sample, or smaller, audience, of about 25,000 households, which represents people from around the country and measures what they are watching.

Today, ratings have become much more complicated. Think about it. When Nielsen started, there were only three television channels and no one could record a program to watch later! Now, ratings have to measure all the ways people watch TV, from DVRs to personal computers.

What Will They Think of Next?

How does this sound?

Paper-thin TVs that you can roll up like a newspaper.

More pixels and brighter colors.

And this amazing idea: Scientists are figuring out how to use brainwaves so that you can change television channels just by thinking about it.

Sound impossible? Well, consider what one person said back in the early days of television: "People will soon get tired of staring at a plywood box every night."

What can you think of that could change the way we view TV?

Want to Work in Television?

There are a lot of ways to get into television depending on what you like and want to do. If you have a local cable station or a school television station, volunteer and try out as many different jobs as you can.

If you like to call the shots, you might make a great director.

You might like the artistic side of television, like computer graphics. You might like to write stories. Or operate cameras. Or, you might want to be a scientist and invent something that we haven't even thought of yet!

A news anchor works in front of the camera.

Floor managers and camera operators work behind the scenes but in the center of the action.

Glossary

assemble (uh-SEM-buhl): to put together the parts of something

consists (kuhn-SISTS): to be made of up of many elements

creativity (kree-ay-TIV-i-tee): ability to use imagination and to think of new ideas

dramas (DRAH-muhz): plays or television programs that are serious rather than funny

encounter (en-KOUN-ter): to meet someone or experience something

equation (i-KWAY-zhuhn): a mathematical statement in which one set of numbers or values is equal to another

interpret (in-TUR-prit): to figure out what something means

range (raynj): to vary within certain limits

sequence (SEE-kwuhns): the following of one thing after another in a regular or fixed order

technique (tek-NEEK): a method or way of doing something that requires skill

technology (tek-NAH-luh-jee): the use of science and engineering to do practical things

theory (THEER-ee): an idea or a statement that explains how or why something happens

transform (trans-FORM): to completely change something

Index

Show What You Know

1. Name two different types of electromagnetic waves.
2. What does frequency mean?
3. What is a pixel?
4. How many colors do you need to create all of the colors you see on TV?
5. Why are television's moving images an example of an optical illusion?

Websites To Visit

https://transition.fcc.gov/cgb/kidszone

http://missionscience.nasa.gov/ems/01_intro.html

www.explainthatstuff.com

About The Author

Judy Greenspan worked in television for many years and always thought TV was a magical invention. Now she thinks the science behind the magic is even more amazing! Judy lives in New York City with her husband and children.

Meet The Author!
www.meetREMauthors.com

PHOTO CREDITS: Cover: boy photos © Syda Productions, TV studio © arrogant; pages 4-5 © marcociannarel; page 6 the word SCIENCE © Monkik, math symbols © Texelart, graphics around the word ENTERTAINMENT © Macrovector, page 7 smoke-filled room © Sergey Shubin, men jumping © Mooshny; pages 8 and 9 diagrams © Designua, bottom diagram page 9 © Arisa_J; pages 10-11 smoky background © arda savasciogullari, smoke machine © nikkytok; page 12 stuntman © Ozphotoguy, page 13 © Syda Productions; page 14 © Mike Focus page 15 woman © eldar nurkovic, weather map © Mike Focus; page 16-17 anchor © Olena Yakobchuk, page 17 duck © Tobias Arhelger; pages 18-19 anchor © eldar nurkovic, meteorologist © Rommel Canlas, reporter © michaeljung, camera operator © eldar nurkovic, TV director © eldar nurkovic, TV engineer © eldar nurkovic; page 22 © Everett Historical, page 23 James Clerk Maxwell © Nicku; pages 24-25 Electromagnetic spectrum © Designua, popcorn © sharpshooter, bags © 3DMAVR, page 25 and 26 waves © Fouad A. Saad; page 26 TV presenter © REDAV, page 27 © Igor Shy; pages 28-29 © Tooykrub; pages 30-31 © ex0rzist; page 32 © Andrey_Popov, page 33 © Yana Alisovna; page 34 top © Everett Historical, bottom photo © gmstockstudio, page 35 rows of potato plants © Alf Ribeiro; page 36 © wavebreakmedia; page 37 © Audrius Merfeldas; page 38 © guteksk7, page 39 "The Voice" © Leonard Zhukovsky, TV page 39 and 40 © piotr_pabijan, leopard page 40 © Ivanov Gleb; page 42 © gooier, pages 42-43 © kentoh; pages 44-45 © withGod, SpeedKingz, ant. All photos from Shutterstock except page 34 2nd down © Fletcher6 https://creativecommons.org/licenses/by-sa/3.0/deed.en

Edited by: Keli Sipperley

Cover and Interior design by: Nicola Stratford   www.nicolastratford.com

Library of Congress PCN Data

STEAM Guides in TV Production / Judy Greenspan
(STEAM Every Day)
ISBN 978-1-68191-708-5 (hard cover)
ISBN 978-1-68191-809-9 (soft cover)
ISBN 978-1-68191-905-8 (e-Book)

Library of Congress Control Number: 2016932586

Rourke Educational Media
Printed in the United States of America, North Mankato, Minnesota

Also Available as: